How to Speak Like a Native
and Finally Beat Your Accent:
Ultimate Accent Reduction Guide

Anthony Frazier

Table of Contents

Learning a foreign language takes time and effort. As soon as you are ready to take on this challenge, you will be faced with several important issues. Often one of the major issues is how to speak like a native and to finally beat your accent. It's all well and good to learn the precise pronunciation of a word, but if you are still coloring the word with your accent, people will know you aren't from around here!

The excitement of knowing another language might be shadowed with the uneasiness of the moment when you try to pronounce words and phrases in a more native-like manner, but fail to do so because no one ever showed you how. In this eBook, we will show you how to finally overcome this obstacle and speak freely and confidently without getting frustrated.

The Benefits of Learning a Second Language

Though it is sometimes really hard to speak like a native in a foreign language and to finally beat your accent, learning a second language can provide you with any number of benefits. Let's first take a look at just what the advantages of mastering a second language are:

1. You can travel the world and meet new people

One of the most interesting benefits of learning a new language is that you can travel around the world freely without worrying about communication issues. You have the chance to meet new people both when learning in a group and when traveling. People usually get more open and friendly when you speak their language.

Besides, when you a foreign language or even multiple foreign languages your options for traveling destinations become greater. It is easier to visit a country and to enjoy your stay there if you know the language. The local people will appreciate that you can speak their mother tongue and it will open up new opportunities for you to learn more about other people's lives and cultures.

And as you know, the world is full of interesting and extraordinary cultures that are so different from each other and sometimes so close to each other at the same time. Knowing foreign languages lets you discover more and see the world from a different perspective, from a fresh angle. Believe me, not everyone has the chance to see all of this, to enjoy and understand the lives of others, or know about their history, philosophy, and their way of living and loving. People who have the chance to travel the world have a greater appreciation for the finer things life has to offer.

Culture is not only about history and lifestyle; it is also about the literature, the way of thinking, the way of communicating that other parts of the world have. A whole new world will open up to you as soon as you start speaking in another language and traveling to the places where that language is exists as part of a culture. Thus, to sum up, you will receive the following benefits from knowing a foreign language:

• Travel and meet new people
• Learn more about other cultures
• Open up a new world for yourself

2. Your brain energy is boosted

Because a foreign language is a whole new complex system that includes grammar, vocabulary, as well as different rules and structures, your brain has to retrain itself to think. It has to absorb and assimilate all of it. As a result, your brain starts working more intensively, and your cognitive thinking, critical thinking, and problem-solving skills begin to evolve.

When speaking in a foreign language, one always has to choose appropriate wording and phrases to express themselves in a meaningful way. Different languages have different nuances, idiomatic expressions, and meanings. Hence the speaker has to choose words and structures from the variety that they may know and negotiate the meaning before using a word in a sentence or a phrase. This involves massive problem-solving processes and needs practice and more practice.

3. Your memory is enhanced

The more you use your brain, the better it will serve you. Learning a language doesn't just involve being able to use different structures, rules, words, and sentences, it also involves remembering how to use all the aforementioned things. That is why people who master multiple languages usually recall names, directions, and places better than people who master only their native language.

One more thing to note regarding multilingual people is that different studies show that people who know more than one language have very sharp minds, i.e. they can notice things better than monolinguals.

4. Teaches you how to multi-task

Multitasking is something that is crucial in this rapidly evolving world. Knowing a foreign language will provide you with the chance to learn and to practice multitasking. People who know multiple languages are used to switching from one language to the other. This, of course, involves complex cognitive processes that demand intensive brain work. People who are used to this can multitask in other spheres of life as well. On the other hand, multitasking is a rather stressful activity if you are not used to it in different activities, including mastering languages.

5. Ensures brain health and sharpness for a longer period of time

According to a study by National Geographic magazine, multilingualism can help avoid Alzheimer's disease and dementia for several additional years. To put it more simply, the study suggested that multilingual people experience these medical conditions nearly four and a half years later than monolingual people do.

The research states that the reason for this is that speaking in more than one language allows for processing information in a variety of ways since the number of neural pathways have to increase in the brain of a multilingual person. In addition to all of this, the study proves that regardless at what age the language learner is, they demonstrate acute attention and perceptiveness.

6. Your first language improves

We hardly ever think before we utter a word or a phrase in our mother tongue. We use the grammatical structures and the vocabulary that we have built up over years, and we do so automatically. However, when learning a foreign language, we start comparing it with the one we already know. As a result, we start paying more attention to the grammar, vocabulary, punctuation, and structure of our native language. This experience provides us with the opportunity to improve our mother tongue as well. As a result, we become better communicators, listeners, and editors. These skills surely help us in our everyday life.

7. You become good at other subjects too

Learning a new language helps improve your performance in other subjects too. Different studies suggest that multilingual people get high scores on various standardized tests, as well as listening and comprehension exercises, as compared to monolingual people.

8. You get better career opportunities

Employers like multilingual employees. For you this means you will have a greater number of career opportunities with multiple languages. The majority of employers think that multilingual employees add value to the workplace and that their skills are vital for an organization or a company.

As a result, according to your Curriculum Vitae if you master more than one language then you are already a competitive job seeker and a potential employee.

• The following are the advantages that employers will get by hiring a multilingual employee:
• People who know multiple languages are usually easy to communicate with
• Multilingual people can understand clients and partners of different nationalities and from different cultures
• Multilingual workers are able to multitask and to notice the details
• People who master more than one language are more open to learning new skills

In this world of startups and various businesses, employers are always seeking out aggressive representation of their businesses. Only an individual with a sharp mind and the ability to multitask can help businesses grow. Most multilingual people DO possess these key skills. Multilingual employees will always be needed in a workplace to bridge the gap between the cultures of different partner organizations and their members.

9. You come to self-discovery and you gain self-confidence

When a new skill is added to your skillset, you start feeling more confident in yourself. Mastering a new language is also a skill that you can add to the list. The confidence that you will gain when you master a language will surely attract other people to you. Confident people are always more appealing since they look more open and friendly to others.

In addition to all of this, knowing a new language is an achievement that everyone can be proud of. It is a very satisfying feeling to know that all your time and efforts have paid off. That is why I would also suggest that learning a foreign language is a way to relax and to find inner peace. When you take the time to listen to and understand other people, you start thinking about your own self as well. This is an interesting path to self-discovery and self-realization. In other words, you not only learn more about others, you also start exploring yourself and your inner world.

10. It becomes easier to learn another language

After you learn a new language, it becomes several times easier to learn another one. The thing is that by assimilating sentence structures, rules and syntax of one language you automatically generate newer tactics and methods to easily absorb other rules, and structures as well. Your brain becomes used to identifying new methods of learning and breaking down the process of language learning into steps.

In this way you are becoming able to learn more and more languages more easily over time. Different linguistic structures gradually become familiar for you and your brain starts to improve its work of assimilating a new language day by day.

As a conclusion, we should acknowledge the importance of learning a new language in this constantly changing world of ours. Bilingualism and multilingualism are a must these days since the rapidly growing economy needs more flexible workers who are able to multitask in stressful situations and who are able to create the necessary bonds with international partners and clients. If we want to be more integrated and connected with the global society, we should, first of all, know how to communicate with them. The most powerful way of communication still remains verbal communication carried out through different languages. Hence, the more languages you know, the better you will be able to feel as a member of the world in general.

The Influence of the Mother Tongue on English as a Second Language

The mother tongue or the native language is the language that a person speaks as a dominant language. When someone starts learning a new language, the mother tongue may influence the new language in several ways. As a result, the language learner may feel reserved and stressed due to that influence since it may show up in their patterns of writing and speech. Let us now consider several examples where the native language influences the foreign language.

In most cases, the mother tongue influences the way you, as a learner of a new language, use grammar and how you structure a sentence. For example, many people try to translate expressions and idioms from their native language to English. As you know, when people translate fixed expressions, those expressions hardly ever make sense. Each language has its own unique language structure and speech patterns. Try translating "hit the nail on the head" literally into Spanish, for instance, and then ask a native Spanish speaker if the translation means anything to them at all. How about "by the skin of my teeth" or "bite the bullet". How would those turn out in French? How about Russian?

It is sometimes really hard to identify the native language influence since the speaker might not have learned the correct grammar rules or expressions. It should also be noted that different native languages get influenced by English in different ways. That's why we cannot simply make a list of all the common mistakes that non-native speakers make when talking in English. Following are the things that might be influenced by the native language:

• The sentence structure and word order
• Syntax

• Grammar rules (verb forms, adjectives and adverbs, tenses, and mood)
• The selection of vocabulary units, words, expressions, and idioms
• Punctuation
• Pronunciation of different words and sounds

The point with pronunciation is really important. There are languages that lack some of the sounds that make up the English alphabet, and vice versa. For example, Germans sometimes confuse "w" with "v" and pronounce a word like "well" as "vell". The French and the Russians are not used to pronouncing the "h" sound properly. Russians generally pronounce the combination "th" in English words either as "d" or as "z". Vowels may pose a problem for a native Chinese speaker, because of the vast difference between Chinese vowel sounds and English vowel sounds.

Some more examples of native language influence include the following:
1. The language learner might not distinguish certain English sounds due to their native language and, accordingly, might not be able to pronounce them in English.
2. The language learner might substitute several native language sounds with those that seem similar (but not identical) in English. For example, the Russian sound "r" can be used instead of the English "r" etc. The Chinese usually substitute their "ei" with the English "e".
3. Usually, the language learners add unnecessary vowels either in the middle or at the end of a word that is difficult for them to pronounce due to the many consonants in it.
4. The language learner may bring their native language stress to the new language. As a result, their words might sound odd with unfamiliar emphasis and difficult to understand.
5. Another scenario connected with the issue of stress is that the language learners might be unable to not stress the

unstressed vowels. If this occurs, double-stress can be heard in a single short word.

6. The language learner may also bring with him the usual tone of voice, sentence speed, and intonation of his/her native language to the foreign language. The same about the voice and the way your mouth works when pronouncing different sounds. For example, several languages involve a little nasality while others do not have that feature.

To sum up, the whole idea of mother tongue influence is that the sounds of your native language seep into your new language, and this can be for a variety of reasons. For example, you might not have listened to enough English speech, or you might not have spoken much in English, or no one has ever tried to correct your pronunciation or other language errors in general. Mother tongue influence can, of course, be fixed through hard work and practice. Hence, if you as a speaker feel that you do not sound correct and you understand that you should do something with your language to make it sound more English-like, you should follow our tips on eliminating the native tongue influence and finally beating the accent.

What is an Accent and do I Have One?

Sometimes it is really hard to notice whether you do have an accent or not. At least, for you it is. The majority of people who learn English think that they do not have an accent yet they come from a variety of cultures and speak different languages that surely have some influence on the new language they are learning. But the question is why don't people notice they still have an accent? The reason for this is because they become so concentrated on the content of what they're going to say that they become distracted from its form and the way it all sounds. Let's look at several facts regarding your accent:

The accent is everywhere

Anyone speaks with an accent, whether they realize it while walking around their hometown or not. For example, when you learn to speak in standard American using the same tone of voice, with word stress and pronunciation like the people speaking this language do, your speech will become easier to understand. As soon as you get rid of your accent, people will no longer ask you to repeat words and phrases in order to understand what you are saying. However, this does not mean that this standard American English is not an accent. It is the accent of North America which might be hard to understand in the south or in other countries where English is being spoken as a mother tongue with a different accent.

And you may not hear yours

As I said above, it is normal to not notice your own accent. But what is not normal is not even trying to improve your accent regardless of how well you speak English. It is very much like cooking. You might think that you are cooking quite well until your partner says that the dishes you cook are sometimes really salty. It's the same with your accent. You might not notice it until someone tells you about it.

One reason why we might not notice our own accent is that as we grow older, our brains start narrowing down their perception of different sounds. For example, a little child may feel the difference between the different pronunciations of "R" than a grown up individual. So, here is the truth we should deal with.

It depends on who you socialize with most

Usually, the individuals who most feel that they need to improve their pronunciation and to eliminate the accent from their speech are those who socialize a lot with native English speakers. Through comparison, they see that their English differs from others' in many ways, and, accordingly, the need arises to improve the language. Additionally, those people who do realize that they have got an accent try to resemble the native speakers. That's why their accent is milder as compared to other people's accents who don't come to this realization.

Hence, if you want to finally beat your accent, you need to spend a lot of time socializing with and talking to native English speakers rather than your non-native English peers.

You can get rid of it if you want

Everyone can get rid of their accent if they want to. You need to practice more and to use the right tools and techniques for doing so. Below is a section that will provide you with useful tips on how to beat your accent and what tactics to use. There is a variety of things you can do to finally beat your accent. Make sure you follow these tips if you really want to speak like a native English speaker.

22 Things to do to Start Speaking like a Native Speaker

A priority for all language learners is to start speaking like a native speaker in the foreign language they are learning. This includes speaking fluently, without any major pauses, and speaking without an accent i.e. in a language that is free from any influence of your mother tongue. The things that I suggest to do are simple and easy. Some of them you should do before you actually start speaking and others can be done while you speak. All of these are steps to help you start speaking in a more confident and fluent way without an accent. Here we go:

1. There is no magic: only hard work

When learning a new language, you should understand that there is no magic bullet or a button you can press to learn it all immediately. You need to practice, and practice again. There are different methods to help you eliminate your accent and your native language influence but all of them require practice. Some methods may turn out to be more effective than others. To be able to speak like a native English speaker you should concentrate your attention on the four aspects of the language:

1. Speaking
2. Writing
3. Listening
4. Reading

If any of these elements is missing from your practice, you won't be able to master the language like a native speaker. Of course, since we are talking about the accent, you should concentrate more on reading, listening and speaking activities.

Note that different techniques appeal to different language learners. Some people are good at memorizing words. Others like to converse a bit while others prefer to listen to English speech more to be able to speak flawlessly. The process of learning a language and becoming proficient in a language will take some time. Thus, you need to make patience your weapon and practice as much as you can because, as the saying goes, "practice makes perfect".

2. Fill in the emptiness

When during a conversion you are asked a question and you don't know how to answer it, you can just ask another question or use a sentence to let your conversation partner know that you either cannot find proper words to explain your ideas or you simply did not understand what they are saying or asking about. You can use the following expressions to express this:

• How do I say?
• What can I say?
• I'm not sure how I can explain this.
• It is difficult to explain.
• I really don't know what my answer to this question can be.
• I don't know where to start.
• I am not sure I know the answer to your question.
• How can I make it more understandable?
• How do you say it in English?
• Where to start?
• I am not sure I understood your question.

Another important thing is to fill in the silence with sentence fillers. For example, if you are telling someone about something and you feel you do not remember a word or a phrase or you cannot make up a meaningful sentence at that moment, what should you do? The answer is as simple as this: try to fill in the emptiness with some sentence fillers. You can use the following:

17

- That's a good question!
- "Um", "er", "ahh" (although overuse of this one can make you sound very non-native)
- How do I say this?
- It is kinda (kind of)....
- Lemme think a bit (let me think a bit).
- How can I put it right?
- That's interesting!
- Funny!
- Nice!

3. Speak while thinking and then speak again

When you are asked something and you need to give an answer, you can use some expressions and sentences before actually giving the answer. This will help you think about your answer and will keep the other person busy while you are generating the actual answer. For example, you can use the following sentences before coming up with the answer:

- My opinion on this topic is certain.
- I have thought a lot about this and I have found that....
- From my viewpoint....
- In my opinion....
- The first thing that comes to my mind when I hear something like this is....
- I do not have any idea about it, but....
- As far as I know....
- As far as I remember....
- The first thing that comes to my mind....
- I'll check that information and will let you know more about....

4. Be a little bit tricky when asking for clarifications

Don't use this one a lot. It can bore people and really turn them off from speaking to you. However, you can still use it from time to time especially when you feel there is no other way to give yourself time to think and to come up with an answer. The scenario is the following: you get a question you need time to think on. You can use the following questions and expressions to send the question back to your conversation partner and to gain time to think about their question:

• I am not sure I understood what you mean by saying…
• Did you mean…. (or)….?
• What should I understand by…. ?
• Did I get you right? You mean….
• Can you give me an example?
• Do you already have an answer to this question?

5. Explain words from your native language, if ever used when talking in English

It is a common thing for beginners to use words from their native language when speaking in a foreign language. It is even common for intermediate level learners. So, don't worry about that. Instead, make sure you explain the word that you just used. For example, you can use your native language word and then say:

• It means that….
• The meaning of it is that….
• I cannot say it in English but in my language, it is this, which can be explained as….
• The approximate meaning of that is….

Also, native English speakers are not afraid of using some vague words and phrases before they actually say something worthy. So don't be afraid to do the same thing. Following are some words and expressions you can make use of:

- I think….
- I suppose….
- More or less
- I guess….
- To me….
- Things like that
- Stuff
- Pretty nice
- Cool
- I'd never imagine
- I'd say
- Stuff like that

6. Prioritize the way you speak, not what you are speaking about

This tip might sound somehow odd to you; however, if you want to get rid of your accent and feel confident when speaking English, then you need to concentrate on the WAY you say something instead of WHAT you say. At the first stages of speaking a new language, try to use only those words, phrases, and expressions that you are sure about. For example, opt for easier expressions that you know 100% well and leave more complex structures for future use. Practicing little by little will help provide you with more confidence to go on with the rest. Also, note that it is better to pronounce words and phrases in a slow manner and a moderate pace to be able to avoid both grammatical and pronunciation errors.

7. Use English in your daily life

You want to learn a language and get rid of that accent? Use the language. Speak in English during the day as much as you can. It is better to speak English on a daily basis for at least fifteen minutes than to do difficult exercises and to practice vocabulary 1-2 hours a week. Even if you live in a country where no one speaks English, you can practice English or listen to English speech daily. Following are several ideas for you:

• Watch English movies and cartoons
• Read the news in English rather than in your mother tongue
• Start thinking in English and translating words and phrases from your native language into English
• Read books and watch movies in English

8. Balance the aspects of the language that you are practicing

If you want to speak like a native, you need to not only speak English but also listen to it when others talk, read lots of materials in English and try to write in English as well. Do not practice speaking exercises only. Take the time to watch movies and to listen to podcasts. In other words, balance the aspects of the language since each of them is responsible for several skills that will help you master the language like a pro.

9. Practice English in a variety of contexts

As I said above, you need to practice not only speaking but also reading, writing and listening. In addition to this, you should practice the language in a variety of contexts. Do not stick only to books and formal language, try to find ways to listen to and speak in more colloquial English. The language that is being used in the street might differ largely from the one that can be used in a workplace, and even at home. So, you need to find ways to make yourself familiar with all the contexts. The contexts that you might consider for your language practice and exercises include:

• Formal and non-formal

- Fiction and the real world
- Lectures and small talk
- Academic and comedy

In order to master the language fully, you should read academic texts and research articles but also listen to various types of songs or watch movies. Just feel free to make your learning experience more diverse, and fun!

10. Start thinking in English

No one can start thinking in English instantly. You need to learn to do that step by step. Here are some steps you can take:

1. Start thinking about separate English words and phrases, e.g. when you want to say something, think how it would sound in English
2. Go deeper and think about whole sentences in English
3. Then, go wild and imagine entire dialogues in English

Thinking in English is a great way to improve your English without worrying about your mistakes and pronunciation errors in front of other people. The more you speak in English to yourself, the better you will be able to master it in the future.

11. Paraphrase. Try different words and expressions

As soon as you feel confident in pronouncing several sets of words and phrases, start paraphrasing whatever you are going to say. If you feel you are going to pronounce a word in the wrong way, just try to find some other word to substitute for it. Let us consider several examples:

- Instead of saying *"The ideas are rather controversial, I do not know how to describe them in a more comprehensive way"* you can say *"The ideas differ from each other greatly and it becomes hard for me to explain them"*.

• Instead of saying *"This risk management software turned out to be surprisingly efficient"* you can say *"I am surprised at how effective this software for risk management is"*.

• Instead of saying *"The managers take pains to distribute the work between the employees and to make sure that each of them presents a substantive demonstration of their own assignment"* you can say *"The managers work hard to give work to every employee and to make them show the tasks they completed in a simple and meaningful way"*.

12. Listen to everything and everyone you can

Before you learn how to speak properly like a native speaker does, you should learn to listen. English is a language of similar sounding words. Is it "police" or "please"? "Draft" or "draught"? "Aren't" or "aunt"? "Some" or "sum"? You should listen to English speech as much as you can to be able to hear the difference between such words. You can learn to listen more accurately from the following things:

• Movies
• Songs
• Podcasts
• Listening exercises

You can find either listening exercises or authentic English audios/videos on the web. Ted is an ideal tool to help you explore the world through the speeches that successful people make and through the variety of English accents that you can hear. The more accents and varieties of English you hear, the better you will feel the difference between a pure English pronunciation and the one that is influenced by the speaker's native language.

Also, you can find online platforms to watch movies in English and to listen to the news.

13. Record yourself and listen to your speech

Of course, it is a good idea to listen to other people speaking in English but it is also useful to record yourself and listen to your own speech too. I would suggest not only recording your voice but also your face when speaking in English. You should see what gestures and mimics you use when speaking. This will help you improve your pronunciation since English is not only about sounds but also about gestures and the expression of your face. You can use various online tools and programs to record yourself on a camera. For example, you can use Screencastify or some other program either for your PC or your smartphone. The easiest way of recording a video of yourself is, of course, doing that with your phone. As soon as you record yourself reading something or telling a story, start comparing the recording with something similar. See how you and other people pronounce the same words and expressions. Consider whether there are too many differences between your speech and the speech of a native speaker. If there are, work to correct them.

Also, you can try to record yourself when repeating a native speaker's words and sentences. After you finish the recording, again consider checking the similarities and the differences of pronunciation. Try again as many times as needed to make it perfect and to sound just like the native speaker does. Also, you can ask someone to listen to your recording and the original version to see whether you really sound like the original version or not.

14. Take into consideration how your lips move when you speak in English

When speaking a language, make sure you move your mouth and the lips in the right way. This will greatly help you to pronounce the words correctly. One way to notice how your mouth moves has been discussed above. That is to record yourself when reading a text or when saying something. Another way to see how your lips move is to just use a mirror. Look at the mirror and try a monolog. Watch other people either on TV or in person to see how they are talking in English and how they move their lips to pronounce specific words and phrases. This will help you notice the difference between your pronunciation and theirs. Also, you can search the web to find pictures and even videos that show how your mouth should move when pronouncing specific words and phrases. 3D animations can also be highly useful when it comes to seeing how your mouth should move to pronounce the words correctly and to sound like a native.

15. See how you move your tongue

Another important body part that is responsible for correct pronunciation is your tongue. Depending on how it moves between and over your teeth, one can determine whether you are pronouncing it right or not. Sometimes, the tongue plays a greater role in helping pronounce the words in a correct way than your lips do. Some non-native speakers usually fail to pronounce the sounds "L", "R", or "TH" in the right way. For example, when you pronounce "L", your tongue must touch the upper part of your mouth and should be behind your front teeth. You can practice the word "level" to feel where your tongue is when you pronounce the "L".

Let us consider another example: when you pronounce the sound "R", your tongue must not touch any part of your mouth, it just needs to be pulled a little back. Try pronouncing the word "reservation" to see where your tongue appears when pronouncing the word. And finally, when you pronounce the sound combination "TH", you tongue must simply rest between your upper and bottom teeth. Try practicing the word "thrive" to see where your tongue is at the moment of pronouncing the word.

If your tongue is not in the aforementioned places when pronouncing these sounds, then your words will not come out sounding right. Try to match your tongue's movements and its position to the descriptions given above.

16. Pay attention to the stress

In English, words can be stressed in different ways. If you put the stress in the right place, you will sound more like a native speaker. Stress is put on to show that some sounds in a word and some words in a sentence are more important than others. Following are several rules on English stress that you should bear in your mind:

• Word stress is put on the vowels only
• One word cannot have more than one main stress, nut it can have a secondary stress
• Several two-syllable nouns and verbs have different stresses while written in the same way e.g. PRESent (noun) vs. preSENT (verb)
• In longer words, usually the second or the third syllable from the end is the one being stressed e.g. geoLOgic, teleVIsion, serenDIpity

Though these are some general facts, there are lots of exceptions. So, you must try to feel what to stress and what not to stress in a word or in a sentence. If you think you cannot feel the stress, don't worry about it. You will get used to it if you listen to English speech as much as you can.

Sentences in English are also stressed. As said above, some words turn out to be more important in a sentence as compared to others. Sentence stress is logical; in other words, it depends on what you want to say and what you consider important in your speech. Reading out loud and listening to different dialogues will help you understand the principles of sentence stress and use it in a correct manner.

17. Find someone to practice English with

It is a good idea to find a native English speaker to help you practice the language. Nothing can be more rewarding than speaking to a native speaker to improve your language. There are different Language Exchange portals and websites where you can find people to chat with. My Language Exchange is one such website where people from all over the world are registered. You offer a language you know well for a language you would like to study and then you find people with interests that match yours.

Practicing with a native speaker will provide you with the chance to practice what you already know and to learn new things as well. Of course, it would be great if you had a real (not a virtual) friend to talk to you in English, but if you do not have one or if you cannot visit a country where English is spoken as an official language, then you could find some alternative ways of getting in touch with native speakers.

18. Read in a loud voice

Read much, read often, and do it in a loud voice. Being able to read fast in English is one of the ways to help you become a more natural English speaker. You need to simply read aloud for some 15-20 minutes every day. When you are reading, try to be as clear and easy to understand as possible. Additionally, set a goal to read faster and faster every time. After you repeat this exercise for several weeks, you will notice how fast you started to read. Your reading will certainly affect your speaking too.

19. Start using contractions; they're awesome!

As you might have noticed, native English speakers love using contractions both in writing and in oral speech. This is done mainly because people find it easier to pronounce two words when they can pronounce just one. This will give you the chance to sound fluent and native-like. Hence, make sure you say "let's" instead of "let us" or "don't" instead of "do not", or "aren't" instead of "are not". You can search the web and find different lists of contractions that you can make use of in your everyday speech.

20. Prepare a script of what you're going to say

Even small talk and similar other occasions might need to be prepared beforehand if you are new to English. Create a script of what you are going to say. This will help you feel more confident in yourself since you will be able to eliminate the awkward silence and the shy pauses that so often occur during a conversation. Having a plan or a general structure of what you are going to speak about will help you generate newer ideas more quickly and easily. This way, you will maintain control over the situation and will be satisfied with your performance.

21. Learn a new word per day

Use a dictionary to learn a new word every day. When you look up the meaning of a word in the dictionary online, you also have the chance to listen to the audio indicating how the word sounds. Using a dictionary to learn new words might seem an old way of enriching your vocabulary; however, it is useful in many respects:

1. You learn the spelling of the word
2. You learn how it should be pronounced
3. You see in what contexts it is usually used

There are many online dictionaries and dictionary apps that you can use either on your PC or smartphone. Following are some such dictionaries:

• ABBYY Lingvo Live
• Thesaurus
• Oxford Dictionaries

22. Do interesting stuff in English

If you think that reading English texts is boring, you might consider doing some interesting activities in English. For example, you can try some cooking lessons in English or you can join an English book club to read English books first and then discuss them with the club members. Just make sure you choose something that really interests you and start doing it in English.

At the end, I would advise that you stay positive and be confident in yourself. It will take less time to become proficient in English than you imagine. Practicing and using the right techniques will surely lead to the completion of your goals. Also, remember that to be a good communicator, you need not only pronounce all the words correctly but also be able to use grammar and vocabulary properly. If you speak slowly and confidently trying to use word stress and sentence stress and paying attention to your grammar and intonation, you will already make a huge step forward towards the realization of your goal of beating your accent and speaking like a native speaker does.

Want to speak well? Listen!

The number one thing to do to be able to speak well in English is to listen to English speech. In other words, if you want to speak better, you must learn to listen better first; odd, yet true, right? Thus, in this section, I will go deeper to provide you with several listening tips and resources that will help you become a better listener and a better speaker accordingly. Here we go. These are fourteen tips to improve your listening skills easily and without frustration.

1. What about a TV show or movie series in English?

It is a good idea to start watching a TV show in English. Choose one TV show every month and start watching it right at the beginning so as not to miss a thing. By following the storyline and the acting of the characters, you will be able to get the idea of the whole show even if you think you do not understand most of what is being told there. By listening to a variety of accents and speech types, you will be able to determine which is more like the native English and will be able to imitate it over time. I would suggest you watch the following TV shows:

- Blue Bloods
- The Tyrant
- Sherlock
- Fargo
- Batman: The Animated Series
- Friends

Hopefully, you will find a TV show that you can get mad about. As soon as you find one, you will spend a lot of time watching it. As a result, your pronunciation will improve and you will become a more confident English speaker.

2. Listen to something on a low volume

Find a podcast or a video online, turn it on, keep the volume low and try to figure out what is being said. This will make your attention become more acute. As a result, you will be able to understand what people say more easily in real life situations.

3. Listen to something in the background

Find a Ted Talk or a YouTube video online and try to listen to it while you are doing something else such as cooking, running, riding a bike, or even reading something. This will save you time in practicing English and you will get used to English speech.

Also, you can find a text and the corresponding audio and try to listen to it and read it simultaneously. The same about the Ted Talks; most of them have subtitles. You can switch them on to be able to see what the speakers say. This way you will learn how words sound in real life as compared to the way you used to pronounce them during your English lessons.

4. Try to listen to the same thing several times

Listening to the same thing several times might seem boring to you. However, this will help you notice the details as you listen to the recording over and over again. With every single time you press "repeat", you pay attention to minor details that you didn't notice the last time. This way, the pronunciation of several words and phrases will be fixed in your long-term memory. Thus, take your time to practice repeating what you listen to.

5. Audiobooks are awesome; turn them on!

If you are a book lover, then you will probably like this method to practice listening. You can find a free audiobook from the Open Culture website or you can buy one. There are also lots of mobile apps that provide free audiobooks. Make sure you listen to it everywhere: in a bus station, while driving back home, when having a bath, when eating your dinner etc.

Audiobooks are especially useful since they include a really wide range of vocabulary and sentence structures. Also, the intonation and the word and sentence stress used by the audiobook's reader are really awesome from the viewpoint of the correct pronunciation and punctuation.

6. Listen to a song and work with it

In some countries like Finland and Sweden, children study English by listening to songs and then practicing grammar and vocabulary through the lyrics of those songs. Songs are really one of the most engaging and fun ways of becoming familiar with a language. By singing along, you will improve your pronunciation and will be able to feel the rhythm of the language. If you are listening to a song and you feel you do not understand some of the lyrics, just make sure you find the lyrics on the web (it's easy, just type the song's title in Google) and start singing along.

7. Take an online English lesson

You do not necessarily have to pay for taking an English course since there are plenty of tutorials and video lessons in YouTube and similar other platforms. Watching these tutorials might be useful especially for beginners. If you feel you have problems understanding what other people say, then maybe you should start with English language tutorials to be able to pronounce, at least, the easiest words and phrases correctly and to the point.

8. Try to copy someone else's way of speaking

Choose someone who speaks English very well. This could be an actor, a friend, or a politician. As soon as you choose the person you are going to "copy", listen to something they say (choose a speech that lasts for a few minutes) and try to copy what they say by repeating both their words and the intonation. Imitation is a great way to reach the desired tone of voice.

Right at the beginning, you might sound rather silly to yourself. However, as time passes, you will notice that your speaking has improved considerably due to these imitation games.

9. Try to listen to something with your peer

Find a friend who also wants to improve their English speaking skills and offer to practice together. Choose a short audio or a video and listen to it first. Then start asking each other questions about what you have listened to or watched. This activity will provide you with the opportunity to check each other's pronunciation and to fix each other's errors if you make any.

10. Listen only for specific details

When you are listening to an audio or you are watching a video, make sure to pay attention to specific things every time. For example, with one audio you can concentrate your whole attention on the use of definite and indefinite articles, with another audio/video, you can pay attention to the word stress or some other aspects of the language. This will give you the chance to throw a closer look at different aspects of a language. As a result, you will sound more accurate when pronouncing similar words, phrases, sentences, and texts.

11. Listen to something and then transcribe it

This exercise is a nice combination of listening and writing (note-taking) activities. The idea is to listen to a short video or audio about 3-5 minutes long and to write down all the words that you hear. Of course, this exercise will take a lot of time but it is worth it since you will pay attention to every single word you hear. If the audio or the video has a script, then you can check your transcription with the help of it to see how many words you missed or how many of them you have misheard and miswritten.

12. Try to figure out what a child says

Because children have got their own English, it is sometimes really hard to understand them. By trying to figure out what they are saying, you will be able to concentrate your attention on common misspellings and mispronunciations that adults may also have.

13. Listen to automatically generated speech

When you read something and there is no audio for it and you want to listen to how the words and the sentences in that text are pronounced, you can use any "text to speech" program to help you turn the text into audio. The computer will pronounce the text for you. Though it may sound a little bit odd, it will be useful for you to listen to the pronunciation and word stress.

14. Listen to someone who has problems speaking in English

Remember, we were discussing that people sometimes do not hear their own accent. That is, they do not imagine how oddly they pronounce words and sentences. In order to find out whether you are among these people, try to find someone who speaks really bad English and listens to them for a while. When a person is unsure about their own speech, they use lots of fillers and sounds in their speech unconsciously. It is really important that you know these sounds for what they are and avoid using them when speaking.

To sum up, these are the things you should consider if you want to improve your spoken English through performing listening exercises:

• Watch TV shows, movies, and cartoons in English
• Listen to audios, podcasts, audiobooks, and Ted Talks
• Listen to something on a low volume or something in the background
• Listen to the same thing several times a day in a row
• Listen to a song and try to transcribe it and then sing along
• Watch English tutorials
• Repeat what others say during a speech (copy intonation and stress)
• Practice listening with a friend of yours
• Pay attention to the details when listening to something
• Listen to children and those people who are beginning speakers
• Listen to computer-generated pronunciation

At the end, remember that you should find the balance between all your daily activities. Include English in your daily routine. Learning and living must be incorporated to make the process of learning a language a much more pleasant activity. Also, it will be great if you get a buddy to practice with. If you cannot find a native English speaker, at least find someone who wants to improve their spoken language and beat the accent, and start practicing.

15. Great Resources to improve both Listening and Speaking Skills

After you found out what you should do to improve the listening and speaking skills, it is time to look at several resources that can help you accomplish your goals.

Ted Talks

I have mentioned the Ted Talks programs several times within this manual. The idea here is that you can watch a variety of speeches by different researchers, experts, and entrepreneurs from all over the world. You can find talks with subtitles in over 100 languages. Ted Talks will provide you with the chance to learn new things and to listen to English speech at the same time. You can also find a lot of interesting stuff to read on their blog.

Breaking News English

This is a free and printable platform where you can find lots of useful and interesting stuff to read. You can choose the level of your English proficiency and start practicing going up and up from one level to the other.

Tools for Life Chating

Watching how native speakers talk is a great way to start resembling them and getting more familiar with the language. You can use the following tools to chat live with native English speakers:

1. Google Hangouts
2. Periscope (Here you can search different places on the map and see what live streaming different people have. This is a great way to listen to authentic English speech.)

3. Tango is also a great tool for live conversations
4. Online TV and Movies in English:
5. Netflix provides you with the opportunity to watch TV shows and movies in English. However, it is a paid service and may have different restrictions and limitations in different countries. At the same time, it is worth giving a try.
6. Hulu is another paid website that streams popular shows in the US. Again, depending on what country you are in, you might need to use a Virtual Private Network to be able to access the website. Hulu also has got a wide variety of movies in English.
7. Fandor is also a paid service that provides movies in different languages.

Online Radio

As you may already know, one can listen to the radio online as well. Following are some websites where you can listen to English language radio:

- Listen Live Europe
- Talk Zone

BBC English Learning

This is a portal that belongs to the BBC website. It is meant to help people learn English. You can find different levels there and different interesting articles to read. Additionally, quizzes games, videos and grammar exercises can also be found in this interactive portal. It is free and you can surely benefit from it to improve both your listening and speaking skills.

Quora

Quora is an alternative platform to help you learn English. People ask and answer questions here. It is interactive, fun, and easy to use.

Elllo.org

This is another website that will help you with your spoken English. You can take different English lessons or simply watch videos. The most important thing here is the so-called mixers which are interactive audios where several people try to answer the same question. By listening to such audios, you will be able to improve your spoken English and gain confidence to speak like other learners do.

The British Council

The British Council provides a vast variety of useful articles, exercises, online games and much more. You can even download PDF questions, exercises and articles to improve your English further.

Urban Dictionary

If you think you are good at English but you cannot pronounce those slangy American words and phrases, then this website is for you. You can search words here and you can also just scroll the page and see what new American colloquialisms you can learn for today.

NPR

NPR is another website for those people who want to learn American English. Here you will find lots of news and interesting stuff that is only in American English. Mostly upper-intermediate and advanced learners can use this website.

5 Minute English

This website shows how fun language learning can be. With its numerous grammar and vocabulary games and quizzes, it will help you improve your English speaking, writing, listening, and reading skills up to any level you desire.

18 Short Tips to Help You Gain Confidence in Yourself and Fight On

1. When speaking, never be afraid of making errors. Instead, be confident in yourself and stay strong.

2. Start living in an atmosphere where English dominates; listen to everything and everyone that is English and stay focused to get the idea of what they are saying.

3. It is better to practice every day for fifteen minutes than once a week for a few hours.

4. Make sure your family members and your friends support you in your endeavor of improving your spoken English and getting rid of your accent.

5. When trying to improve you speaking skills, never forget about the writing, reading, and listening skills that must be developed.

6. Do not be lazy, use a dictionary and keep a notebook to write down words that you are not familiar with.

7. Try to learn new words in context since it will help you to remember those words for a longer period of time.

8. Take a test every two weeks to determine your progress and to see what you should work on more.

9. Remember that learning or improving a language is not a one-time goal. Instead, you should view it as a long-term endeavor.

10. Divide your long-term goals into smaller short-term objectives and reward yourself every time you complete an objective.

11. Choose the right methods for you to improve your intonation and the speaking skills. You know the best methods which suit you and which are useless.

12. Get help either from your English language teacher, or a friend, or a native speaker, or someone who has done this before. Never be afraid of asking for advice.

13. From time to time conduct a revision of things you have learned in the past.

14. Do spend some money to get paid subscriptions for English language TV shows and movies.

15. Read books and listen to audiobooks since they are useful for broadening your horizon and for enriching your vocabulary.

16. If you are a beginner, you can start with children's books and do not forget to talk to English speaking children.

17. Speak English to whoever you can, whenever you can, and how often you can!

18. Be crazy enough to think in English and talk to yourself in English.

Conclusion

Believe me, it is never too late to start improving your spoken English and beating your accent because you are never too old or too young to start doing that. And do not find excuses to not speak like a native; you yourself feel how cool it is to sound like a native English speaker. Instead, just enjoy the process of learning new things. Make practicing English a daily activity like sleeping and eating. And never give up, stay positive. If at some point you feel you are about to give up, just look back at the learning materials that you used long ago to learn the language; this way, you will see how hard a path you have passed already, and how far you have come.

Also, every time you feel like giving up, make sure you ask yourself what you need to improve your spoken English for. I am sure you will have multiple of answers to this question. One such answer can be to make your life better, or to make the world a better place by sharing ideas and feelings with people from other cultures, or to have greater career opportunities. Motivating, isn't it? Then, find the courage in yourself to always fight on to achieve your goals and to make all your dreams come true.

If you liked this manual, feel free to share it with your native English peers and with your friends as well. We would also like to get feedback and comments from you regarding the materials we have shared with you. Were they useful? Did you use them? Please, feel free to share your experiences and opinions with us.

Thanks

Thank you for reading the How to Speak Like a Native and Finally Beat Your Accent: Ultimate Accent Reduction Guide. I wish you the best of luck and hope this book will help you to reach your goal! If you have the time and inclination, please consider leaving honest review on Amazon or Goodreads. Thank you and good luck.

Made in United States
Orlando, FL
11 December 2022

26147729R00026